Adventures in Hearing God's Voice

By Joshua Hutto

CreateSpace Publishing

**ISBN-13:
978-1974402489**

**ISBN-10:
1974402487**

Acknowledgements

    This book was the product of countless conversations with brothers and sisters in Christ, and I could spend a whole chapter on names and influences that helped it become a reality. Nonetheless, I do have some very special people to thank that made all the difference.

    First of all, thank you Jesus. This book was your idea and you were sitting right next to me throughout this whole process. Thank you to my wife, Amanda, who has supported me during this process in a thousand little ways that will never be seen or enjoyed by anyone but me. Thanks to my Editor Sara, who took this ungainly mix of stories and Bible verses, and shaped it into something people could read. Thanks to my cover designer Andrew for being gentle and creative in everything he does.

    Shout out to all my early readers. Lauren Steffes, you are responsible for a whole chapter of this book! Thanks also to Monique, Lauren Weaver, Anna Beth, and Lylian for providing some great feedback. Finally, thanks to my dad for having the courage to write a book first and for telling me he is proud of me every chance he gets.

Table of Contents

Introduction

Chapter 1 - Is His Voice really for me?

Chapter 2 - The Biblical Context of a God's Voice

Chapter 3 - It is Written

Chapter 4 - The Still-Quiet Voice

Chapter 5 - Our Visual God

Chapter 6 - Dreams

Chapter 7 - His Touch

Chapter 8 - Through His Body

Chapter 9 - Being like Jesus

Chapter 10 - What Now?

Introduction

Jesus is alive. This simple statement is the foundation of this book. He is moving and speaking to His people all over the world, and I have been truly blessed to be chosen by Him as a testimony of His grace. I am a young professional in the medical industry whose only qualification for speaking with authority on this subject is the blood of Jesus. Here, I share a collection of my personal testimonies and simple explanations for some of the ways the God of the Universe has humbled Himself to speak to me.

I make no claim to have discovered a definitive list of the only ways He speaks. Instead, I would like you to think of each chapter as an introduction to a different aspect of the Father's voice. Some of the ways I receive from the Father might be familiar, while others might be new to you. Each of these chapters was written prayerfully in the fear of the Lord, and none of them are based on experience alone. Each concept I introduce in this book has a strong biblical basis that I pull from. Consequently, I am prepared to stand before the seat of judgement with a pure heart.

The purpose of this book is to invite each of you into a personal conversation with the Holy Spirit. I fully recognize this is a place of anxiety and fear for many believers because we face an enemy who is the chief among deceivers. Reading this book will by no means end his attempts to tempt and deceive you; But we have been given a sure-fire way to reveal any deception that would come against us:

> Dear friends, do not believe every spirit, but test the spirits to see whether they are from God, because many false prophets have gone out into the world. This is how you can recognize the Spirit of God: Every spirit that acknowledges that Jesus Christ has come in the flesh is from God, but every spirit that does not acknowledge Jesus is not from God..." (1 John 4:1-3, NIV).

So, I exhort you to take anything that you are unsure of and test it against this verse. The Holy Spirit has a favorite subject; it's Jesus! It is His nature to glorify Christ, and He will never do or say something contrary to His nature.

All of the blessings and trials that have molded me into the man I am today begin and end with His voice. It is my sincere hope as you read this book, your faith is ignited to believe in the **God who speaks**. It does not matter who you are, God wants to have a conversation with you! He doesn't speak in mysterious riddles or vague signs; He speaks clearly and simply. You don't need a degree to know God intimately. No amount of experience is needed for a life of daily communication with Jesus. In fact, Hebrews says, "No longer will they teach their neighbor, or say to one another, 'Know the Lord,' because they will all know me, from the least of them to the greatest" (Heb. 8:11). This promise is for everyone, yet most people I talk to in the church regard *hearing from God* as some sort of mystical and possibly blasphemous activity. It is my experience and sincere belief Jesus died so you could talk straight to the Father and hear Him reply.

This book is an invitation to begin the most engaging and life giving conversation of all time. In the following chapters, I have laid out some basic ways God speaks to His people. In most chapters, I have included a prayer that I invite you to pray with me. Each prayer is carefully crafted as a starting point for to receive more of what I describe in the chapter, and I encourage you to join me in each prayer of activation in these facets of God's Voice.

May the God of hope fill you with all joy and peace as you trust in him, so that you may overflow with love by the power of the Holy Spirit (Rom. 15:13).

Chapter One

Is His Voice really for Me?

For most of my childhood, I was raised by an abused mother and abusive stepdad. My mother would never defend us, and my step dad would yell at us for hours, many nights keeping us up until 1:00 or 2:00 a.m. We were constantly doing chores or participating in "family time" which always turned out to be endless lectures or some sort of MTV special we did not want to watch. Looking back, it is hard even to imagine how many nights my sisters and I would try to do all we could to avoid getting in trouble, only to fall short and endure whatever punishment was slotted for that night.

Yet it was in this very context that I can first remember God speaking to me. I was about eleven years old, trying to fall asleep in my windowless room under the stairs (yes, Harry Potter and I had a lot in common) when I suddenly got hit with a wave of sadness. It struck me that none of my friends at school were facing the same problems I was dealing with. I found myself overcome with self pity. Crying into my pillow, I moaned out my complaint, regretting my terrible family situation.

Then in the midst of my melancholy I heard Him speak:

"Forgive him."

The voice was distinct and unique in my mind, un-asked for and completely off track with my self-pitying thoughts. The thought was so novel that I stopped crying immediately and thought through how it could be possible. As a child, I was not told to go to church by my father and forbidden to go by my stepfather. But I did know that forgiveness was God's territory, so without missing a step, I replied.

"Okay, God. I'll try."

My situation with my stepdad did not change for years, but I distinctly remember after each especially difficult night with him I would always make sure to speak to the same voice I heard that first night.

"God, help me to forgive my stepdad... I want to forgive him. Help me."

I didn't know it, but these prayers would become foundational parts of my relationship with God. At that age, I wasn't reading the Bible and I didn't attend a Sunday school. I was just a little boy who needed help. *And help came in the form of the Helper Spirit.*

You may have heard stories like this or even read some of God's interactions with His people in the Bible and thought, "*That's cool, but I know that stuff is not for me.*" I know I have personally heard that phrase from many people. When confronted with concepts like visions, hearing the voice of the Lord, receiving dreams from God, or anything else in that realm, I understand how lack of personal experience can encourage us to believe some things are only for *other* believers. Maybe this belief is not conscious, but it manifests itself in small thoughts like: "I love listening to him speak. He really hears from the Lord," or "Well, of course, he saw miracles happen; he was addicted to drugs, and then gave his life to Jesus."

These thoughts, or thoughts like them are very cleverly crafted by the enemy to convince each one of us that some special quality or experience is required to really *know* God. This is the foundation of the deception of the religious spirit of striving which whispers to each of us, *"Intimacy must be earned."* Yet the good news of the gospel is that the only qualifier for each of us to have intimate experiences with God is the work of Jesus on the cross. By the blood of Jesus, we can approach the throne of God and, if it is true we have been given permission, we should not sneak forward hesitantly but boldly go before our Father with much rejoicing.

"You have been blessed with every spiritual blessing in the heavenly places in Christ Jesus" (Eph. 1:3). In Jesus, we have access to the full power and work of the Holy Spirit. The same relationship Jesus shared with the Father is available to us through the redeeming work of the Cross. He offers us this relationship with open hands, asking that we give up our lives so we can fully access His.

The key to understanding our place in the wonderful outpouring of His love can be found in 1 Corinthians:

> Just as a body, though one, has many parts, but all its many parts form one body, so it is with Christ. For we were all baptized by one Spirit so as to form one body—whether Jews or Gentiles, slave or free—and we were all given the one Spirit to drink. Even so the body is not made up of one part but of many.
> Now if the foot should say, "Because I am not a hand, I do not belong to the body," it would not for that reason stop being part of the body. And if the ear should say, "Because I am not an eye, I do not belong to the body," it would not for that reason stop being part of the body. If the whole body were an eye, where would the sense of hearing be? If the whole body were an ear, where would the sense of smell be? But in fact God has placed the parts in the body, every one of them, just as he wanted them to be. If they were all one part, where would the

body be? As it is, there are many parts, but one body (1 Cor. 12:12-20).

Look down at your hand… go ahead. Wiggle your fingers and take some time to appreciate the immense complexity of the mechanics of that one movement!

When you moved those fingers, you used: 27 bones, 123 ligaments, 34 separate muscles, and 48 named nerves. While for you this movement seemed almost effortless, the level of coordination involved is actually staggering.

Paul's metaphor is just as relevant now as it was then. The psalmist says it so well, "I will praise you because I am fearfully and wonderfully made" (Ps.139:14). Both our individual bodies and the Body of Christ were crafted by God to be masterpieces. They are both made up of millions of intricate and unique parts designed to work together towards a single purpose.

Even something as seemingly mundane as a hand is a masterpiece of beauty and grace. As we give up our lives to follow Christ, we are all "baptized by one Spirit so as to form one body." Each of us has an amazing, unique role to fill in this body. There isn't going to be another made like you for the rest of eternity. It is our greatest joy to find what we were made to do, and do it well! "For we are God's handiwork, created in Christ Jesus to do good works, which God prepared in advance for us to do" (Eph. 2:10).

No one can do what you were made to do like you can! It is my sublime joy to know so many brothers and sisters who know their place in the body and live it out with excellence. These people are the happiest, most peaceful people I know. The same joy and contentment is for all of us to experience in Christ Jesus! We have but to find our place in this beautiful body of His and live fully in His love. If you are wondering how to do that, we can look again to the body for some amazing answers.

Each part of the body is tied to the rest by a long string of messenger cells called nerves. It is through the nerves that one part of the body can talk to another. Just as all roads lead to Rome, every nerve pathway leads to the brain. In one way or another, the head of the body is actively involved in making sure that each part of the body is moving in concert with the others. If there is an infection in the body, the head turns up the heat with a fever to burn that sucker out. If you break a bone, the head is immediately informed and makes sure the rest of the body protects the broken part as much a possible. In the same way, Jesus Christ is actively fulfilling all of these duties and more throughout the whole body!

Colossians says: "And he is the head of the body, the church; he is the beginning and the firstborn from among the dead, so that in everything he might have the supremacy" (Col. 1:18). Christ is the head of this body, and He has plans -- plans to prosper you, not to harm you. In all things, He will lead you and help you fulfill your purpose as a part of His body.

It is time to stop sacrificing our destinies on the altar of comparison and jealousy. So many of us are giving up our own amazing and unique callings because it, "doesn't look like what we expected"; or, "it's not as glorious as the person up on the stage." It does not matter what you think disqualifies you from hearing His voice or living the supernatural life He has for you. You have been bought and paid for on the cross. This is the very definition of *redeemed*. "You have been set free from sin and have become slaves to righteousness" (Rom. 6:18). You now have a new owner. God, Righteousness Himself, is your master now; and there is no master like Jesus. His "yoke is easy, and His burden light" (Matt. 11:30).

He gave you what you need to succeed and to have joy. We were not meant to just float around on this earth, pursuing the desires of our flesh, never truly feeling satisfied. We were made to receive the messages that *the head*, Jesus, is sending us. He spoke and is still speaking to us through the nerves of the body, the great connector Himself, the Holy Spirit.

Paul urged the Galatians to do the exact same thing when he said, "So I say, walk by the Spirit, and you will not gratify the desires of the flesh" (Gal. 5:16). If you have been blessed to be rescued from your sin by Christ, then you are His. He is not just a sin removal service you can call in once a week to help you with your guilt. He is the King of Kings and the Lord of Lords. He is calling us, His church, to higher things, to true obedience. If you are His, you can no longer skate by on what you hear Him speak through others. We each have to come to know His voice for ourselves. Jesus said: "My sheep listen to my voice; I know them, and they follow me" (John 10:27).

Actively listening for His voice is the foundation of following Jesus. In the same way that the quality of a foundation defines the quality of any building, the depth of our communication with God defines the level of fruit each of us can bear in this lifetime. It is no longer a question of whether or not this whole *hearing the voice of God* thing is for you. You have been called and chosen by God Himself to fulfill your destiny, and you cannot ignore it any longer. Pray this prayer with me as we all seek a greater knowledge of His heart towards us, His children:

Father, I surrender to you. I lay down my ideas of my identity and open my heart and mind to the renewal of your Word. Show me who you are and who I am in you. Teach me what it means to be yours while I walk with you here on earth. Amen

Chapter Two

The Biblical Context of God's Voice

"Call to me and I will answer you and tell you great and unsearchable things you do not know" (Jer. 33:3).

We serve a God who speaks. Each of us who believe acknowledge the validity of this statement. However, the question much of the western church wrestles with is whether God speaks to us *personally*; and if so, how does he choose to communicate?

To find the answer to this question, we can begin with the very nature of the Bible. The Bible is divided into two parts, the Old Testament and the New Testament. Both are full of the teachings and stories of people who heard from God. The myriad of ways each person received a message from God are amazingly diverse, and this book would have to be much longer if I wanted to do a survey of each of them.

There is a reason Revelations describes his voice as sounding like *many waters* (Rev 14:2). The wonderful mystery of God's voice can be found in the diversity of flowing bodies of water throughout creation. From the incomprehensibly deep boom of the mariana trench to the twinkling trickle of a mountain brook, water is producing music which reflects the full breadth of the sound spectrum.

He is wildly creative in the ways He chooses to communicate, and there is no better record of this variety than the books of the Bible. From the terrifying clouds of smoke and fire on Mount Sinai (Exod. 19) to the almost comical choice of speaking through the mouth of a donkey (Num. 22), God refuses to be limited by how he chooses to communicate. The reality is God will pretty much speak through anything and anybody. In fact, for fun, let's make a short list of some times God spoke in unexpected ways:

- A bush (Exod. 3)
- A whisper in the middle of three natural disasters (1 Kings 19)
- A cloud tower (Exod. 13)
- Caiaphas, the guy who was responsible for killing Jesus (John 11:50)
- A vision about pigs on a blanket (Acts 10)
- A dream about cows (Gen. 41)
- A dream about grapes (Gen. 40)
- A rug (Judg. 6)
- A belt (Jer. 13)
- That guy in the hair shirt (Matt. 3)
- A rainbow (Gen. 9)

These are just snapshots into ongoing conversations between God and His people. There is no other God like our God. He is Emmanuel, God among us. He is Powerful, Brilliant, Funny, Righteous and Faithful. Yet we cannot learn these things just by reading about how He acted with people thousands of years ago. We were created to personally know God.

In Psalms, He differentiates Himself from all other gods. "They have mouths, but cannot speak, eyes, but cannot see. They have ears, but cannot hear, noses, but cannot smell. They have hands, but cannot feel, feet, but cannot walk, nor can they utter a sound with their throats" (Ps. 115:5-7).

Have you ever thought about having a God who can smell? It is mind blowing to think that throughout the Bible, God talks about smelling things! Once you start to look, you find verse after verse of God expressing His feelings and desires in a way that is tangible. He clothes His bride Israel in the desert (Ezekiel 16). He protectively shelters us under His wing (Ps. 91). Time after time the Bible reveals a God who is real in every sense of the word. He is not an abstract idea or a really good set of morals. He is not a figment of our imagination, or a statue in our buildings.

He is the God who walked with us in the Garden. The God who spoke with Moses face to face. He is the God who actually wants to be with His people. There is no greater display of this than when He sent his Son, Jesus. Jesus asks Philip, "Don't you know me, Philip, even after I have been among you such a long time? Anyone who has seen me has seen the Father. How can you say, 'Show us the Father'? Don't you believe that I am in the Father, and that the Father is in me? The words I say to you I do not speak on my own authority. Rather, it is the Father, living in me, who is doing his work" (John 14:9-10).

Jesus is not His own person; rather, He was the full display of God's character on earth. Therefore, we know God's heart by looking at Jesus' heart. Think about how Jesus would speak to practically anybody. He would touch anybody. There was no exclusive group that earned the right to hear His secrets. Instead, he would go out to the hills and preach, and anyone who wanted could follow. He was *accessible*. He is the example we must keep in mind when we begin to think about beginning a conversation with God.

He wants you to speak to Him, and He wants you to hear what He has to say in response. All throughout the Gospels, people would just walk up to Jesus and ask Him a question, and he *always* responded. He didn't always say something that was immediately understood. In fact, He usually didn't say what people wanted to hear. But He spoke! And He is still speaking. "These are the things God has revealed to us by his Spirit. The Spirit searches all things, even the deep things of God" (1 Cor. 2:10).

Right now we can't speak to Jesus face to face; instead, we speak to Him through the Holy Spirit. At first, I thought we were getting the short end of the stick, I mean can you imagine getting to have lunch with Jesus? You could ask Him all of those burning questions or get Him to pray for you. Instead of having to come up with awkward ways to sneak God into conversations with my unbelieving friends, I could have just said, "Hey, have you met Jesus? He is a pretty cool guy." and then casually gesture to my living, breathing Savior. He could take it from there.

In fact, that is literally how Philip introduced Nathanael to Jesus. But the Bible has a very clear stance on which is better for the church between the man Jesus and the Holy Spirit. "But very truly I tell you, it is for your good that I am going away. Unless I go away, the Advocate will not come to you; but if I go, I will send him to you" (John 16:7).

The word *advocate* in the New Testament in Greek is *parakletos*, which basically means one you call to your aid, an intermediary or representative. What Jesus has sent, we have a responsibility to receive. In fact, the very purpose of His ascension to heaven was to send the Advocate Himself to dwell with us. Your relationship with the "Advocate" is not meant to be confusing or deeply mystical. It is meant to be an active daily experience that deepens your connection with Christ and our Heavenly Father. The picture we have of the first century church is a picture of a community of believers actively being lead by the voice of this Advocate. Paul has dreams leading him to the correct cities. Peter has visions given to him by the Holy Spirit that change the course of the church's theology forever. The whole book of Revelation is one big recorded vision!

Now it is true Jesus will one day come again, and as a church intimate with the Holy Spirit, we will have become the *Spotless Bride* John speaks about in Revelations. But as a church, we are not meant to wait for this fullness huddled in the dark! We have been given the Holy Spirit as a seal of this promise, just like an engagement ring is given to a future bride as a sign of the coming covenant relationship. To ignore the gift of the Holy Spirit is to waste a chance to grow in the knowledge and fear of the Lord this side of heaven.

The Holy Spirit was given as an avenue for us to deepen our understanding of what it means to know God. Paul says in Ephesians: "I keep asking that the God of our Lord Jesus Christ, the glorious Father, may give you the Spirit of wisdom and revelation, so that you may know Him better" (Eph. 1:17).

In our New Covenant, the only way we can deepen our relationship with God or *know Him better* is through the Holy Spirit who searches all things, even the deep things of God. The Holy Spirit is searching these things out for us! He was sent here to lead us, guiding us along the straight and narrow way in our relationship with God. Or as it says in John 14:26: "But the Advocate, the Holy Spirit, whom the Father will send in my name, will teach you all things and will remind you of everything I have said to you."

He is here with us right now. Even as you read this book, the Advocate is with you. He is longing to reveal the deep things of God to you, the secrets and hidden things of the Father's heart. He wants to unravel the mystery of the cross for each one of us, until its truth is powerfully displayed in our lives. Yet the practical ways He wants to do this are so often shrouded in mystery and very infrequently taught about in church.

No longer can we sit idly by, content to believe in Jesus but not know and be known by Him. All around us, God is doing what He promised in Joel 2:28: " And afterward, I will pour out my Spirit on all my people. Your sons and Daughters will prophesy, your old men will dream dreams, your young men will see visions. Even on my servants, both men and women I will pour out my spirit in those days."

The Holy Spirit is available to all of us, young and old, male and female. There are no exceptions. To follow Jesus is to be intrinsically linked to Him through His Spirit on earth. The days are passed where you get all of your knowledge about God from a preacher or a really anointed spiritual leader. God can and does want to speak to us through these people, but as it says in Hebrews: "No longer will they teach their neighbor, or say to one another, 'Know the Lord', because they will all know me, from the least of them to the greatest" (Heb. 8:11).

God wants to reveal Himself to us and through us in awesome and unique ways. He wants to rest with you in the secret place of your soul, just like He did in the garden with Adam. This is a space He wants to clear out in gentleness and love, removing all the weeds and rocks that are the voices of fear and pride in our own lives, filling it instead with such a wonderful collection of truths and facets of His character. He wants to reveal Himself to you and in so doing, show His love to every tribe and nation on earth!

Every time God connects with man in the Bible it is for the purpose of revealing His character. From Adam to John the Revelator, God endeavored to display His character to us in such a manner that we could choose Him through love. Yet how can we choose what we do not know and how can we know what we have not experienced? It is in the receiving of this radical, personal love that we are equipped to testify to the nations. "Very truly I tell you, we speak of what we know, and we testify to what we have seen" (John 3:11).

Access to personal experiences with God's love did not end with the last page of Revelations but continues today in each of our lives. His love cannot be contained or overcome. As you make the choice to turn towards Him everyday, the love He showers on you will impact everyone around you. In fact, He is speaking that love over you right now, and the purpose of this book is to help you to become a child who hears and delights in their Father's voice every day.

Chapter Three
It is Written

Without question, the greatest blessing the church received after Jesus and the Holy Spirit is the Bible. In my own testimony, the great constant in my walk has been the Bible. To this day, I am constantly drawn by the Holy Spirit to the scripture, which Paul says, "is God-breathed and is useful for teaching, rebuking, correcting and training in righteousness" (2 Tim. 3:16). This great love for scripture was awakened in me at eighteen years old, in an old storage room in my freshman dormitory.

During winter break my first year of college, I had an encounter with God that totally changed the course of my life. I had been addicted to pornography for years, and I knew as a follower of Jesus, I had access to freedom. I just could not seem to hold on to it for any period of time. I was in a revolving door of temptation and failure. This consistent sin in my life humbled me deeply, until one day I found myself asking God what I was so afraid of. Why did I keep running away from Him? What He said marked me deeply and has shaped my walk ever since.

"Son, you are afraid of intimacy with Me. You think that I will not be enough, so you go to other places to fulfill your desires. But I promise you I am enough, and if you give up everything to be intimate with Me, I will fill you with love. At My right hand, are pleasures forever more. And I promise you they are much richer and life giving things than pornography and masturbation."

His words utterly changed me. I came back to college on fire to know who He was and what He wanted from me. I threw myself into worship and prayer, hungrier than I had ever been to know what it meant to follow Him. During this time, I began to see people around me make decisions to follow Christ; perhaps the most surprising of which was my best friend, Alex. Alex was, and I quote, "the strongest atheist I had ever met." He was mildly interested in my beliefs and had even asked me some questions as a part of a religious survey he was doing to learn more about Christianity.

One day, a few weeks into the spring semester, I walked into a room to find Alex reading the Bible! I walked in, my Bible already in hand, to do the same thing. As I sat down, I casually opened my Bible to join him. I knew that, like a unicorn, I was probably never going to see this again if I spooked him, so I quietly went about my business.

My *play it cool* act lasted about thirty seconds before I blurted out, "Dude, why are you reading a Bible?"

He looked up at me with a small smile and said, "Well, I think I am going to try this whole God thing."

"Like Jesus and everything?"

He laughed at my obvious excitement and took a deep breath before replying, "I am not sure, I think I am going to read this thing all the way through, and once I meet Jesus, I will decide if I am going to follow Him."

Taking that astounding statement in stride, I did the next best thing I thought a Christian could do. "Hey man, how about you come to church with me this week! You can learn a ton about God and the people are great."

He didn't respond immediately. Instead, he looked back down at his open Bible and said, "I don't actually feel that comfortable letting someone I don't know teach me about Jesus and this book without having read it for myself."

I didn't love that answer, thinking that anybody who tried to get all the answers before they went to church would never make it to church. My face probably showed it too because he quickly followed up his statement with, "Look man, I am already on the Numbers chapter and I really like it so far. I promise I will come with you to church after I am done."

"Numbers?" I said horrified. Then I quickly explained, "You don't have to read that one! Nobody does really! Why don't you start with the Gospels and move on from there?"

"Man, are you kidding me? I love Numbers -- I mean each one of these guys had a story with God, and God thought it was so important that He recorded their names for all time in this book! I have only been reading for a couple of days but I definitely know I am going to make it all the way through. When I read this book, it feels like I am a stone in a river, slowly being made smooth by the water that is rushing all around me."

What Alex said shocked me. Until then, I had read my Bible just like any other Christian, mostly hopping around, sometimes finishing a whole book but never really having an experience like Alex was describing. Without ever having been in a church or reading the Bible himself, Alex was experiencing what Jesus talked about in Ephesians 5:26; He was being "washed by the water of the Word."

This experience rocked me. After class that day, I opened up my Bible to Genesis 1 and prayed, "Father, I have read so many books, but I have never read Your book! Make it come alive to me, so I can read it for the amazing and engaging story it is."

Then I began to read. As I read through the first five books of the Old Testament, I began to feel like I was in the story itself, learning about this God who had encountered man through the ages, building us up into the Bride who will one day marry His Son. If I had any questions or was curious about a specific person in the Bible, I would just stop and pray and ask God to show me more about who David was or what the heck Ezekiel was seeing in the first chapter of his book. The experience was utterly transformative.

One of my favorite book series as a kid was Harry Potter. I identified with the main character in many ways and longed for the significance Harry found in his fight against evil. While these books impacted me greatly, I cannot imagine what it would have been like to read them with my own personal JK Rowling right next to me. I mean, every time a character died or a funny joke came up, I could pause and share the moment with the author herself!

This doesn't begin to describe the experience I had reading through the Bible for the first time. I wasn't reading a book about God, trying to find clues to His character. I was reading "His-story" with Him! When we got to the point where Jesus died in Matthew, I cried because in that moment, I felt the sadness He felt losing His Son. The words written in the Bible had become more than dead things written long ago for historical purposes. The words I read were alive, washing over my heart and healing my soul.

My life is filled with wonderful encounters with God's Spirit. And it is not because I have found the perfect formula to spiritual excellence that says: e*very day you must have one hour of prayer, read two Bible chapters and tell one stranger about the Gospel of Jesus Christ.* I have heard many of my spiritual heroes talk about such habits and disciplines as one of the keys to their relationship with God. Yet each time I tried to replicate one discipline or another, I was always met with failure.

Even though my story contains failure and weakness, I still find myself constantly being spoken to, touched and blessed by God as He perfects His strength in me. This steadfastness on His part has finally started to reveal to me the true secret of a steady, unshakable relationship with God. He made the first move on the Cross. If we trust and wait on Him, He will always finish what He started in us.

"We love because He first loved us" (1 John 4:19).

This verse is not just a description of our first commitment to Him when we decided to give our heart to Jesus. This statement is a beautiful summary of the Gospel and our entire walk with Christ! We cannot love at all without first receiving His love. This is why John always calls us *the Beloved* in his book. In order to walk with God, we must *be loved* first.

This principle absolutely applies to growing closer to God through reading the Bible! As wonderful and attractive as reading the Bible two hours a day sounds, any pursuit of God without personal interaction with the Holy Spirit is a waste of time. The Pharisees had pretty much memorized the Bible of the time, and yet they had managed to completely miss Christ! We can and will do the same if we pursue spiritual knowledge for knowledge's sake. This is what Paul is describing in 2 Corinthians. "He has made us competent as ministers of a new covenant -not of the letter but of the Spirit; for the letter kills, but the Spirit gives life" (2 Cor. 3:6).

God is longing to speak to us! He loves His children and wants to reveal His character to us! The Bible is one of His sweetest and most precious gifts in this regard, but we must approach it as children, letting Him do the leading, just like he shows us in Hosea. "I led them with cords of human kindness, with ties of love. To them I was like one who lifts a little child to the cheek, and I bent down to feed them" (Hos. 11:4).

Take some time after this chapter to really lay down your relationship with the Bible and let Him begin to change the way you approach His book -- not as a step-by-step guide or the exhaustive Christian rulebook but as a living breathing message of God's heart for your life. I invite you to pray this prayer out loud as a first step:

Father, I repent for any way I have abused or taken the Bible for granted. Thank you for the wonderful and simple door you left open for me to walk into your heart and spend time with you. I ask that you would draw me through the pages of the Bible into a deeper encounter with you. I lay down all the times I let obligation or guilt force me to read your story and ask that you would renew my mind. Open the eyes of my heart, so that I can be as excited to read your testaments as you were to write them.

Chapter Four
The Still-Quiet Voice

"The LORD said, 'Go out and stand on the mountain in the presence of the LORD, for the LORD is about to pass by.' Then a great and powerful wind tore the mountains apart and shattered the rocks before the LORD, but the LORD was not in the wind. After the wind there was an earthquake, but the LORD was not in the earthquake. After the earthquake came a fire, but the LORD was not in the fire. And after the fire came a gentle whisper" (1 Kings 19:11-12).

So many of us have some expectation of God's voice being exclusively grand or undeniably obvious. When I think of Elijah, I think of a man terrified by the wonders he has seen God do. This man is no stranger to God's power and has seen things we can only dream of. But here in this passage we see a completely different interaction. God was showing Elijah that, while He is a God of splendor and power, He also absolutely speaks in a gentle and quiet voice!

Not only is His gentle whisper present all throughout the Scripture, but it is actually one of His favorite ways to speak! Why? Because this method of communication, more than most, requires faith to hear and receive. When you read something in the Bible, you are guaranteed that God said it at one point or another. There is a level of security in that, and for that reason, the Bible was given to the whole body so that we can all hold in common a record of His voice. The reality and sanctity of the Scripture does not negate our personal revelation of His voice; instead, it supports it and causes it to thrive!

      We are each being pursued by the Holy Spirit, and as a result, whether we realize it or not, we are recipients of this gentle whisper all the time! It can come in the form of thoughts that seem more encouraging than normal or desires to do something that seems completely out of place in our pursuit of comfort and security. In fact, these thoughts can many times sound like Bible verses! The fact that good thoughts exist is not evidence of the inherent goodness of humanity, as some would have you believe. They are the echos of the Holy Spirit inviting you into a conversation.

      Jesus Himself was constantly living out the reality of a daily conversation with the Father. We have a wonderful sign pointing to this internal conversation in John:

> "Father, glorify your name!" Then a voice came from heaven, "I have glorified it, and will glorify it again." The crowd that was there and heard it and said it had thundered; others said an angel had spoken to him. Jesus said, "This voice was for your benefit, not mine" (John 12:28-30).

We have this awesome scene where Jesus enters Jerusalem and explains how He is coming there to die when suddenly He interrupts His own sermon and shouts out to God, "Father, glorify your name!" And God actually shouts back! It freaks out the crowd, and people start arguing about what they just heard. Some say it's thunder while others say it's an angel. Instead of clarifying that it was the voice of the Father, Jesus calmly tells everyone, "This voice was for your benefit, not mine." Jesus was speaking directly to us who would come after, letting us know that there was so much more to His relationship with the Father than the big, flashy miracles and thunderous voices.

Later in the same chapter, He expounds, "For I did not speak on my own, but the Father who sent me commanded me to say all that I have spoken" (John 12:49). Jesus confidently declares that not a single word coming out of His mouth is His own. Instead, He claims every word came directly from heaven. There are only a few times in the Gospels we see God speaking audibly to Jesus; yet we are told He is receiving every word directly from His Father. This leads us to realize there is some sort of hidden communication going on between God and His Son. If Jesus was to walk out life in such a way that nothing would be done or said outside of God's direct influence, He would need to hear direction for every step of His journey. Can you imagine having a little ear piece connected directly to heaven you could constantly access? You could get any direction or answer you needed.

This concept is so important that, one of the few times God speaks out loud in a miraculous and obvious way, Jesus goes so far as to say, "This voice was for your benefit, not mine." I love the bluntness of this statement. It is so simple; yet it implies so much. Jesus is the beneficiary of such an endless stream of affirmation and intimacy with His father that when the booming audible voice explodes in response to one of Jesus' requests, He doesn't personally consider it a big deal. I mean, if when I was hanging with some friends, I decided to voice a quick prayer:

"God I ask that you would speak to us tonight."

Then, exploding from our midst, all of us hear this booming voice respond, "I HAVE SPOKEN AND WILL SPEAK AGAIN!"

Not only would it be a big deal to me, but I would probably have a breakdown right there. In fact, good luck getting anything out of me for the next week. I would be a blubbering mess. Yet Jesus had so much confidence and faith in the quiet, private voice He experienced every day. To Him, it made no difference whether God spoke out loud or in the still, quiet whisper.

The relationship Jesus had with His Heavenly Father blows me away. In the face of such radical faith, I can sometimes feel a huge gulf forming between how Jesus walked and what I believe is actually possible for my life. I mean, can anyone really walk just like Jesus?!? But The truth is when I gave my life to Him, I gave up hopelessness and doubt. Now I receive the call John laid on my heart in 1 John 2:5-6. "But if anyone obeys his word, love for God is truly made complete in them. This is how we know we are in him: Whoever claims to live in him must live as Jesus did."

If you really want to obey the Word and love God, you have one calling in life -to live like Jesus lived. You did not receive grace so you could be content as a sinner for the rest of your life! Grace exists so we can walk on earth just like Jesus did. It is the empowering force of the Holy Spirit that enables us to be the body of Christ. This fully includes having a conversational relationship with your Father in Heaven.

Jesus talked this way to the Father every day. Everything He said and heard was filtered through the lens of the Father's voice. And because of this direct connection, He was able to walk in perfect peace and unfailing hope. However improbable it may seem, we are called to live in this same connection with the Father. It's what Jesus died for! So let's discuss some basic starting points to launch you on a journey towards a completely renewed mind filled with the voice of the Father.

Every one of us has thoughts, and these thoughts form into fast moving internal dialogues all day long. These racing dialogues are so prevalent many people have trouble sleeping because their own thoughts are keeping them up! Sadly, most of the *can't sleep* thoughts are rooted in anxiety and are, therefore, from the enemy. This is not really a surprise to most people. Satan has long been attributed the ability to whisper little temptations and fears into our minds. Yet this voice is counterfeit compared to the vibrant, loving influence of God's voice that we have access to in our minds!

I know it sounds crazy, but I promise it is true. When God promises us a renewed mind, He promises He will renew all of the thought patterns and broken ways of thinking that have been established in us by the broken world we live in. For every lie that we battle, there is a full inheritance of love and truth the Holy Spirit wants to unlock for you.

Each of us is engaged in a continual internal dialogue. It is important to realize you are not *talking to yourself*. You are interacting with spiritual forces and concepts that shape your very identity. These internal dialogues are the fruit of a deeper system of beliefs we have built our lives upon. All of us in Christ are in the process of truly choosing to believe what He has said to us. This is where the renewing of the mind comes in. We are not passive spectators in these mental conversations. We are active participants! We have the ability to choose what voices we listen to in our head. In listening, we have the authority to agree or disagree with them. Here is an example of a thought conversation that probably every one of us has had:

"Holy crap, my test is tomorrow! Have I studied enough?"

"*Nope, you are probably going to fail*"

"Crap, I am totally going to fail. I need to start worrying right now and study as much as I can between then and now." Or, "Since I am going to fail anyway, what's the point? I might as well give up now."

This classic example is evidence of the enemy's voice in our lives. He is always accusing and discouraging. His voice always results in death. From the moment he talked Eve into eating some fruit to right now, he tries to make our days as miserable and hopeless as possible. Thank God we have access to a new voice! The voice of the Father is truly powerful and the only source of eternal life.

Paul tells us in Romans: "The Spirit you received does not make you slaves, so that you live in fear again; rather, the Spirit you received brought about your adoption to sonship. And by him we cry, *'Abba,* Father'" (Rom. 8:15). Therefore, we are no longer slaves to the voice of fear! Our enemy can and will try to speak what he wants through our thought life or through our parents and friends, but he is no longer our master. A new voice wants to break into all of our internal conversations with life and love! Let's look back at this conversation; but instead of being slaves to fear, this time we will be children of God:

"Holy crap my test is tomorrow! Have I studied enough?"

"Dont worry son, you studied, and you are ready. Be at peace."

"Okay, Papa, I believe you, and I trust you to be faithful to me."

This second conversation may seem cheesy, but it is right out of one of my early college journals. It is through conversations like this I had access to a completely different college experience than most of my peers. I did not stress about tests, and school did not rule me. Instead, I got to walk in the peace and the joy that was my inheritance. So let's look at how the second conversation stands out when compared with the first.

First, and most simply, where the first conversation resulted in guilt and condemnation, the second called us to be at peace and resulted in trust and intimacy with Him. Luke 6:43-44 says: "No good tree bears bad fruit, nor does a bad tree bear good fruit. Each tree is recognized by its own fruit. People do not pick figs from thorn bushes, or grapes from briers."

The prospect of differentiating between all the thoughts running through your head can be a little daunting at first, but I promise it is much simpler than it seems. Jesus made a way for us to be with Him in this life and the next. That fully includes hearing and understanding His voice. He promised us His way was always simpler and better when He said, "*For my yoke is easy and my burden is light*" (Matt.11:30).

There are no exceptions to this promise, no special cases in which people only hear God in certain complicated ways. God speaks in so many ways, and all of them are simple and clear. It is our job as His children to be constantly crying out, "God, give me ears to hear!" Everyone of us as His followers, have this calling to discern his voice. In His own words, Jesus assures us, "My sheep listen to my voice; I know them, and they follow me" (John 10:27).

It doesn't matter where you are emotionally or where you are in your walk with God; I am here to tell you the good news that God speaks! He is eagerly waiting for those times when you take a deep breath and look to Him. It is then He will whisper something wonderful to you -- something special and perfect that you desperately need to hear.

A few years ago, I was at a charismatic conference with a few friends. Worship at this conference was wild. I spent a lot of time looking around, enjoying all the crazy stuff I was seeing. One particular kid caught my eye. He was a young, stylish black kid probably around 17, and he looked bored out of his mind. Others from his group were crying, praying or even dancing, but he just stood staring off into the distance with his hands in his pockets. In a room where most people were *feeling it*, he clearly was not. Ever been this guy? The one person in the room who seems to not be connecting with God? I know I have.

For some reason, my eyes kept coming back to this kid. After a while, I was not surprised to see him heave a sigh, look around, and start heading for the door. My heart went out to the guy. I knew what it was like to be dragged somewhere by a mom or an aunt and feel uncomfortable the whole time like I didn't belong. But I felt like God had something special for him. It was at this point I heard the whisper.

"Chase after him, son. I want to speak to him."

I, of course, delayed, uncomfortable with the idea of running after some kid I had never met. Unfortunately, comfort has very little to do with obedience. I knew the difference between fear and love, and love was the one telling me to go, despite fear trying its best to dissuade me. So I jogged out of the large conference room and caught up to the kid halfway down the hall.

"Hey man, I was praying and God sent me out here to speak to you."

"Umm, okay," he said, clearly not liking where this was going. He was probably expecting some sort of rebuke from a stranger -- one more weird thing about this weird conference.

So I took a breath, listened for a second, and then spoke. "Look man, God sent me out here because he wants you to hear His voice for yourself. None of this is going to mean anything to you if you are just here for your pastor or because your mom dragged you. Choosing to follow Jesus is so much more than that. He wants to be your best friend, to talk to you every day," I blurted out in a passionate rush.

He seemed to consider my words for a second, and then making a decision he replied, "Okay then, how am I supposed to hear Him?"

I smiled, absolutely sure I was about to see something really cool. "It's really easy. Just ask Him a question. I recommend doing it out loud. Then close your eyes and listen."

He looked at me blankly. I realized he wanted me to give him a question to ask. So I went with one of my favorites, one I still ask the Father all the time. "Try asking Him, 'Father, who do you say I am?'"

So he looked around the empty hall, then squeezed his eyes shut and mumbled, "Father, who do you say that I am?"

In the silence that followed, I got a mental image of something glowing falling out of the sky and hitting Him in the head (I'll cover that in the next chapter). The silence dragged on for about another ten seconds until, knowing he had received something up there, I said, "So, what's going on up there?"

He popped open his eyes, his face relaxing from it's scrunch of concentration with a dejected look of failure I am sure it had worn many times before. "Man, I didn't hear anything."

Smiling because that is the usual response, I replied, "Actually you did." And I described what I had just seen.

He processed what I said for a second and then thought back to the question."Okay, maybe I did. But it can't be from God. It doesn't make any sense."

"Why don't you tell me anyway?" I said, excited to hear what it was.

"I heard…" He exhaled in a long shuddering breath, tears beginning to spill over his cheeks, not quite able to say out loud what was in his heart. "He told me I am a king," he finished in a whisper. Then, as if the words had physical weight, he dropped to his knees and held his hands as if he was holding something. Looking up at me, he asked, "But what does that mean?"

Laughing in delight at how wonderful it was to see a brother get hit by the love of the Father, I knelt down beside him. "Let's ask and find out."

The story goes on, but I want to end it here because we have all we need. We have a young man who was feeling out of place. He was bored, upset and secretly wishing he could have the same connection with God he saw others experience.

I asked the young man to close his eyes and ask out loud because I thought it might help him concentrate on what he was doing, but neither of these things are necessary to hear from God. 2 Corinthians 2:16 says we have been given the "mind of Christ." It is by faith that we receive anything from God. If we have been given the mind of Christ, then it is only by faith that we can live that out in this world. Paul says:"I have been crucified with Christ and I no longer live, but Christ lives in me. The life I now live in the body, I live by faith in the Son of God, who loved me and gave himself for me" (Gal. 2:20).

So let's get down to business. I want you to get out a writing utensil and your journal (or any piece of paper really) and give this a go:

At the top of the page, write: *God, who do you say that I am?* Read it out loud wherever you are and put your pen to the page. Whatever comes to mind, I want you to write down. No matter how Christian cliche or strange. Don't stop writing until you have a good chunk of the page filled.

……….

Now read what you have written a couple of times. Find the Bible references hidden in the text (He loves to do that). Meditate on any of the phrases that really speak to you, and take the leap of faith that you did not make this up. Dare to believe that the God of the universe is having a one-on-one conversation with you! He really is that simple.

Throughout the process, you will probably make some mistakes discerning His voice, and that is totally okay. Just like you would never punish a baby for trying and failing to walk, your Father will never punish you for seeking out His voice. He loves it when we chase after things from Him!

The words of God in Isaiah 55:3 are just as essential for us as they were to Isaiah: "Give ear and come to me; listen, that you may live."

Chapter Five
Our Visual God

Have you ever noticed how visual God is? I mean, think about it for a second. God hardly ever deals with abstract concepts; instead, He is constantly using metaphors and imagery to give substance to the grandeur and mystery of His character! The Bible is filled with passages and stories that provoke our imaginations to begin to grasp the idea of an all powerful Creator God who can be known on a personal level.

Let's take a look at some scriptural examples of Him giving us a way to grasp facets of His nature:

- He describes His love as a mighty flame that cannot be quenched by many waters (Songs of Sol. 8:6).
- He describes us as sheep whom He leads as a shepherd (John 10).
- He describes His Kingdom as an amazing treasure worthy of selling anything to get (Matt. 13:44).

I could go on forever! The point is that each of these descriptions was crafted by the Holy Spirit to help us *see* something. He wants us to be able to testify of a kingdom that we have viscerally experienced! This Kingdom is just like the psalmist described when he penned, "Taste and see that the LORD is good; blessed is the one who takes refuge in him" (Ps. 34:8).

These words in Psalms are more than flowery language; they are an invitation to open our minds and even our imaginations to the Holy Spirit. As our minds are renewed, He wants to build in us an openness to *see* the things of His Kingdom. This is exactly what Paul is praying when he says, "I pray that the eyes of your heart may be enlightened in order that you may know the hope to which he has called you, the riches of his glorious inheritance in his holy people" (Eph. 1:18).

God has been showing Himself to His people for-like-ever! Jesus only did what he *saw* His Father doing. Way before Jesus, Ezekiel saw a bunch of *visions* of Y-H-W-H (the ancient Hebrew name for God), His throne and His New Jerusalem. After Jesus, Peter fell into a trance and *saw* a vision of unclean animals. It was through this vision, all of us Gentiles were confirmed by the Holy Spirit to be allowed to follow Christ. Some of the things God wants to share with you just won't fit neatly in a word or sentence. There is a reason the saying goes *a picture is worth a thousand words*.

Ever since I began learning that following Jesus looked more like a friendship than a religious duty, I have been closing my eyes and seeing fantastic displays of His love in prayer. These images have ranged from meditations on the throneroom of God to out of the box explanations of concepts in the Bible.

Just like the still, quiet voice from the previous chapter, the things I see when I close my eyes have become an essential parts of my daily walk with Jesus. But it is important to acknowledge that we live in a broken world, and more often than not, the images that come to mind as people close their eyes are not great ones. For example, my head is not constantly filled with rainbows and butterflies; I was addicted to pornography for years, and the enemy still sends attack in the form of pornagraphic images to me today.

Most men can empathize with this visual temptation from the enemy. In fact, this is a well-accepted part of the Christian experience in the western church. Yet the area of *image* is not limited to sexual temptation. All of us have closed our eyes at one point or another and seen images of our worst nightmares or greatest weakness. This reality is unavoidable growing up in a broken and sin-filled world. But I have good news, my friends; this is not your destiny! Romans 12:2 says, "Do not conform to the pattern of this world, but be transformed by the renewing of your mind..."

There is new life available to each one of us. In this new life, our minds and hearts are not constantly being captivated by the things of the enemy but by the beauty of the kingdom of God! Here, each time you close your eyes to daydream, you aren't battling temptation; but instead, your mind is filled with good thoughts and wonderful images of the good God has planned for you. This is what Paul is talking about in Philippians 4:8. "Finally, brothers and sisters, whatever is true, whatever is noble, whatever is right, whatever is pure, whatever is lovely, whatever is admirable--if anything is excellent or praiseworthy--think about such things."

So let's try it for ourselves! I want you to ask God another one of my favorite questions: *God, can you show me something about yourself?* I suggest asking out loud and closing your eyes after you ask, just for the concentration bonus you get when you do both of these things. Then take a few seconds and let yourself see whatever image comes to mind.

Every image that crosses your mind is always really easy to discern. The enemy has not changed tactics since the beginning, and our Shepherd is really so much better at leading than the enemy is at deceiving. Take whatever you saw and run it through the same discernment process I described in the previous chapter.

If you find yourself facing a lot of disturbing things as you try to see what God is showing you, DO NOT PANIC. You are not alone! Early in my walk, I began asking Jesus to show me what He meant when He called Himself my husband, and it seemed like every time I would ask, I saw a homosexual encounter between myself and Jesus. I could not get past this for weeks. I felt ashamed and dirty. BUT I DID NOT STOP ASKING!

I wanted to know, and no matter how many times this attack from the enemy would try and steal my attention, I would break it in the mighty name of Jesus and ask again. As I pressed in, I began to see such wonders of revelation from Him -- the kindness He shows each one of us as His bride, the patience that He joyfully accesses every time we fall short. Even through the mess, I began to fall in love with and trust Jesus as my Husband and leader.

The lessons I learned in that season form the foundation of the relationship I have with my wife today. It is under His leadership, following His example, that I can be the husband I am to my wife. I handle every argument between my wife the same way. When I get upset or afraid and I say something out of selfishness, I take a second and remember who I am. I am a son of Jesus and a follower of Christ. Then I close my eyes and ask Jesus what He wants me to do.

Sometimes He will tell me with words, but more often, He will show me an image. I will see me hugging her or He will take me back to a time when I was acting the same way towards Him. He will show me how He responded to me in that time. In this way, I am truly learning to say the words Jesus wants to say to my wife and to love her the same way He would. It is almost as if He is teaching me to grow in trust towards Him when it comes to the way He does things until, "it is no longer I who live, but Christ who lives in me. And the life I now live in the flesh I live by faith in the Son of God, who loved me and gave himself for me" (Gal. 2:20).

Some of the strangest things I have ever received from God came in the visual form. So if you find yourself seeing a lot of weird and difficult things to understand, don't sweat it! If they are not obviously from the enemy, put them on the back shelf, and God will confirm His will or show you any deception the enemy is throwing your way. He is really good at this sort of thing. If what you are seeing feels like an invitation to do something risky, go for it! God really does not mind us making mistakes when we are trying to do His will. We never know what He has planned.

On my very first mission trip, I was in the hostel room with a bunch of people from my college ministry. The lights were out and we were just having a little pillow talk.

The guy leader of our trip rolled over in his bunk and looked at me, "Josh, I think you can read my mail."

At that point, I was only a freshman and had really only been doing the *hearing from God* thing for a few months. So I said, "Thanks man, what does 'read my mail' mean?"

He laughed and said, "It just means I think you can hear from God so well that you could even tell me what is sitting in my mailbox right now..." Then with a mischievous twinkle in his eye, he went on. "Here, I want you to try something. I am going to think of an object, and I want you to ask God what it is."

"Okay," I said, trying not to think too much.

At this point, I knew next to nothing about this stuff; so instead of worrying about failure or the pressure of being the focus of everyone in the room, I just closed my eyes and said the first thing that came to mind, which turned out to be an image from one of my favorite children's books.

"I am not sure if this is right, but I saw a Fire tru-"

Before I could finish, He yelled and jumped out of the bed, flinging on the light and yelling, "Oh my GOD! I was literally thinking, '*firetruck, firetruck, firetruck.*'"

Another person in the room interjected, "What am I thinking?!"

I closed my eyes again and said, "Horses!"

"Nope! 3 balloons!"

I like this story because I did not suddenly develop the ability to read minds, and I certainly was not filled with the kind of faith Jesus had in Luke 5:22 to know the thoughts of the pharisees sitting at the table with Him. I was not confident or experienced. Yet God took the opportunity and the little faith I had to teach me something that totally changed my life. God loves to jump in on us and use our little acts of faith!

In this instance, God used an image out of my favorite childhood book, *The Great Big Book of Everything.* He brought to mind the page showing hamster firefighters saving bunnies in a burning building to turn a normal conversation into a faith building testimony! Although it seems small and silly, this experience really taught me to expect God to speak, no matter how small the situation. So don't discredit something you see because it's strange; instead, try to take things at face value with a simple faith like a child.

> He called a little child to him, and placed the child among them. And he said: 'Truly I tell you, unless you change and become like little children, you will never enter the kingdom of heaven. Therefore, whoever takes the lowly position of this child is the greatest in the kingdom of heaven" (Matt. 18:2-4).

The Kingdom of God is simple, but I can guarantee it is going to look different than you expected. This will be especially helpful to keep in mind in the next chapter because nothing gets weirder than dreams from God.

Chapter Six

Dreams

There is no question that God sends weird dreams to His people. Usually, the meaning of the dream is not immediately apparent, and sometimes it's impossible to search out on your own. In that instance, seeking some wise counsel can be a good idea. You might even know someone who has a gift of interpreting. But for starters, let's look at some of the times God sent dreams to His people in the Bible.

Joseph had a pretty weird dream about a bunch of wheat bundles bowing down to him (Gen. 37). Then later, when he was in jail, he interpreted some strange dreams from a couple of palace workers (Gen. 40). When news of his gift reaches Pharaoh, Joseph takes his dream interpretation skills all the way to the top (Gen. 41). We also see how God uses Daniel in a similar situation in Daniel 2.

In the New Testament, Joseph had a dream that saved his family from the census of Herod. "When they had gone, an angel of the Lord appeared to Joseph in a dream. "Get up," he said, "take the child and his mother and escape to Egypt. Stay there until I tell you, for Herod is going to search for the child to kill him" (Matt. 2:13).

Most of us have dreams, whether we want to or not, and like everything else, God wants to use things already present in our lives to speak to us! When we take a step back and really open our hearts to hearing the voice of God, He will use anything to tell us who He is and how he feels about us. Dreams are no exception! In fact, dreams are one of the most unique ways God speaks to us.

As a friend of mine once said, "I love when God sends me a dream because it is the only time that I hear from Him, and I can't ignore it or get distracted. I am there for the whole message, whether I like it or not."

This couldn't be more true. We are pretty much a captive audience when God sends us a dream. The same is true when we experience attacks from the enemy in the night. All we can do is hold on until we wake up and then process what we experienced with God. Dreams are both a wonderful ministry from God, and in the hands of the enemy, a terrible weapon. Thank God we have the authority to command protection from the things of the enemy, and we have the standing with our Father to request more of His ministry to our hearts through dreams.

Having us as a captive audience means even when we feel like we are not ready to see, God will show us facets of His character that are not as popular as others. Some of my greatest encounters with the fear of the Lord have happened in my sleep. I have literally woken from some of these dreams shaking like Job describes in the Scripture.

> In a dream, in a vision of the night, when deep sleep falls on people as they slumber in their beds, He may speak in their ears and terrify them with warnings, to turn them from wrongdoing and keep them from pride, to preserve them from the pit, their lives from perishing by the sword (Job 33:15-18).

Due to the variable nature of dreams, I decided to stop immediately shutting one out if it was scary or unpleasant. Instead, no matter what I feel about the dream when I wake up, I just ask God.

"Papa, what do you want me to know about the dream I just had?"

Then after He speaks, if I feel like the dream was from Him, I will take the time to write it down and talk with Him about it later. This method has helped me not to miss important messages from God, even those that came in unpleasant packages but bore amazing fruit in my life. Even if I know the nightmare I just had was from the enemy, I will still ask God about it. Some of the sweetest words of encouragement I have ever received from God have come from conversations that started in the midst of terror after a horrifying dream.

There is no way to adequately sum up all the forms a dream from God might take, but I have found it helpful to classify them as if they fall on a spectrum. On one end is the simple straight forward word of direction. These dreams are not terribly hard to interpret. A great example of one of these is when God told Joseph to take his family directly to Egypt.

On the other end of the spectrum is the emotional and metaphorical language God uses to speak to our hearts. The more a dream leans toward this end of the spectrum, the more it is directed at our hearts. A great example of this sort of dream is the rolling barley loaf the Midianite soldier spoke about in the hearing of Gideon (Judg. 7:13). These sorts of dreams usually hide an important message for our hearts. In this case, Gideon was being exhorted in His heart to have courage. Why God chose to use a giant piece of bread to prove to Gideon that He would show up in the battle, I don't know. In fact, most of these types of dreams don't make sense to our logical minds, but through seeking wise counsel and consulting the Holy Spirit, you can unpack the message God has for your heart.

My sophomore year of college, I was burning for the Lord. I went to a service or prayer meeting every night of the week and was involved in several campus ministries. I didn't know it at the time, but I was on the fast track to burning out! Then in the middle of all my business, I had a dream.

In the dream, I was walking along a path. Approaching me from the other directions was an old man I knew was a spiritual leader. As we met on the path, He stopped and looked me up and down,

"You're a good kid, but you could be better."

"What do I need to do?" I said, hungry to know what was required of me.

He reached out, grabbing me by the shoulders and shouted, "REST!" shaking me awake.

For the next few years, I sought the Lord on His rest. I didn't really need to sit with the Lord for a long time to find out what He was trying to tell me for this particular dream. He was just directly intervening in my life with divine guidance. Still to this day, this dream is bearing good fruit in my life, reminding me to always reach for rest first, letting it be the foundation of all I do.

Dreams like this are fun because they are simple, and they usually require a lot less work to understand. But, at least in my experience, dreams like these are much rarer than dreams God sends for my heart. Much more often, I am thrown into the wild adventure of God's mysterious heart for me as I sleep.

The farther your dream is towards this end of the spectrum, the more important it is to write them down. God Himself can be found encouraging different kings and prophets to write down what He tells them all throughout the Bible.

Writing down what God sends you in a dream, especially one that you don't understand, does several important things. First, it is a practical way to not forget what He has said to you, something we have been guilty of for a long time. This is why we see one of the writers of Proverbs pleading with the reader, "Get wisdom, get understanding; do not forget my words or turn away from them" (Prov. 4:5).

I don't know about you, but if I wake up from a dream at 3:00 a.m., I am probably not going to have a long conversation with God about its meaning and impact on my heart. What I can do is muster up the energy to reach over, grab my phone and type up a quick summary I can come back to later.

Second, to write out a dream you believe is from God is an act of faithfulness. No dream is too weird or too small to ask God about, and if you begin by being faithful with little, I promise you will receive more and more specific and impactful dreams. Jesus really clarifies this concept in a parable in Matthew. "His master replied, 'Well done, good and faithful servant! You have been faithful with a few things; I will put you in charge of many things. Come and share your master's happiness!'" (Matt. 25:23). No matter how small a message or a word from Him seems, do not despise the day of small beginnings! Instead, be thankful and faithful with what He is giving you today, and you will receive more tomorrow.

Third, the final thing I believe writing down your dreams does is develop something I like to call *dream literacy*. Repeatedly, in my dreams, I find certain images and people showing up. Upon investigation, I find each of these symbolic images carries a similar meaning. This literacy has made navigating the wide spectrum of my dreams much simpler, but it requires a history with God to develop. Such a history becomes a wellspring of life and testimony, growing your faith day by day as you see Him lovingly lead you in such a supernatural way.

It is usually people who have taken the time to grow a history with God in the area of dreams who become interpreters. We can look back again at Joseph to see a great example of this. Joseph was a dreamer, and even though he knew his dreams were from God, they brought him nothing but trouble in the beginning. Yet God did not intend to waste the messages He gave Joseph. It was through Joseph's history with God that he came to know that every dream has meaning and purpose in God's eyes.

After finding himself unjustly thrown in jail, Joseph's two cell mates disclose their dreams to him: "'We both had dreams… but there is no one to interpret them.' Then Joseph said to them, 'Do not interpretations belong to God? Tell me your dreams'" (Gen. 40:8).

Joseph recognizes the three branches and the three baskets in his cellmates' dreams as meaning three days. This experience doesn't seem to help him at all. The cupbearer is exalted and forgets about Joseph, and the baker is killed. But two years later the Pharaoh has a dream that no one can interpret, and the Cupbearer remembers his boy Joseph. Joseph hears Pharaoh's description of the dream:

> He was standing by the Nile, when out of the river there came up seven cows, sleek and fat, and they grazed among the reeds. After them, seven other cows, ugly and gaunt, came up out of the Nile and stood beside those on the riverbank. And the cows that were ugly and gaunt ate up the seven sleek, fat cows. Then Pharaoh woke up (Gen. 41:1-4).

Joseph relied on his history with God to grow and develop some solid dream literacy. The whole seven healthy cows and seven ugly cows thing is simple to Joseph. He knows there will be seven years of great harvest and seven years of famine. Then of course he is raised up to the right hand of Pharaoh and does a lot of great things for his family.

God has not changed! He is still sending dreams to world influencers today! I would not be surprised if Martin Luther King had a literal dream from the Lord that radically impacted his hope for what America could be.

We have a call on our lives to begin being faithful with what God has given us. He is always speaking, and if you want to begin to experience the God who, "speaks in their ears as they sumber" (Job 33:15-18), pray this prayer with me:

God I repent from any way I have discounted my dreams, and I lay down any judgements or mistakes I have made when given dreams from you in the past. I ask for an open heart and mind to receive things from you in my sleep. Father, I ask that you give me wisdom to discern your will and character in my dreams and help me to be faithful with whatever you give me as I grow with you in this area of our relationship.

Chapter Seven

His Touch

From the moment we are born, we begin receiving communication through all five of our senses, including touch! When our mother kisses us or we feel the strength of our father's arms for the first time, we are immediately receiving vital and powerful messages of love. Their presence shapes the way we experience the world. The baby in an orphanage who learns to stop crying because no one will come hold it, will forever be marked by their experience. Conversely, the baby who is constantly held and lovingly treated will be blessed with a naturally higher self-worth. If these things are all true for our relationship with our earthly parents, how much more so with our Heavenly Father!

Touch is an essential part of any intimate relationship. Nothing communicates closeness like touch, and nothing communicates distance like the absence of touch. Talking to my wife over the phone will never be as good as talking to her face to face; and talking to her face to face will never come close to talking to her while holding her in my arms. These are simple truths of intimacy, yet so much of the time we let the enemy talk us out of this aspect of our relationship with God.

From the beginning, God has been shouting that He loves us and wants to be near to us. Tragically, we chose pride and sin over Him in the garden and separated ourselves from our Maker. Our forms became unclean and unable to withstand the fullness of His glory and righteousness.

The Bible is clear that God's touch is not something to be taken lightly. He is a constant source of warm encouragement and love, but He is also the Righteous Judge who holds preeminence over all things. The way He touches our lives reflects the fullness of His nature. As the psalmist says, "for day and night your hand was heavy on me; my strength was sapped as in the heat of summer" (Ps. 32:4). It can be a heavy and fearful thing. It is for this reason that the seventy elders of Israel refused to approach Mount Sinai. "The people remained at a distance, while Moses approached the thick darkness where God was" (Exod. 20:21).

Now before we judge these guys too harshly, these elders had very good reasons fear and not to approach God's Holy presence. These were the same people that would learn that to send an unclean man into the Holy of Holies was to send him to his death. Only through very specific cleansing rituals was one allowed to approach. "But only the high priest entered the inner room, and that only once a year, and never without blood, which he offered for himself and for the sins the people had committed in ignorance" (Heb. 9:7).

But God was never content with this distance! It was never His desire to allow distance to remain between us. What happened in the Garden was not some cosmic mistake. God knew exactly what it would cost to create a being with free will and He did it anyway. "For he chose us in him before the creation of the world to be holy and blameless in his sight. In love..." (Eph. 1:4).

He loved us with a love that gave us the freedom to run away, and then sacrificed a Son to give us the chance to come back. Jesus provided the blood that lets us enter the Holy of Holies. A great price was paid for you to enter into the presence of our God and Father, and it is a gift that should be cherished and experienced everyday.

Now, what am I talking about when I say "God's presence"? God is, of course, omnipresent; yet for some reason, He allows Himself to be invited into a place, becoming somehow *more present* in that place. All throughout the Old Testament, we see Him choose to dwell or rest in actual geographic locations to meet with His people, just like He did with Solomon:

> When Solomon finished praying, fire came down from heaven and consumed the burnt offering and the sacrifices, and the glory of the Lord filled the temple. The priests could not enter the temple of the Lord because the glory of the Lord filled it" (2 Chron. 7:1-2).

God was already in the temple, but He was not revealed to His people. Then Solomon prayed. In that moment, God peeled back the layers of reality to show them a little bit of what it was like for Him to physically be in a place. In the same way, when the guards and priests came looking for Jesus in the garden, He took the opportunity to give them a small experience of His true authority, showing us that no one was taking His life; He was freely giving it:

> Jesus, knowing all that was going to happen to him, went out and asked them, "Who is it you want?"
> 'Jesus of Nazareth,' they replied.
>
> 'I am he,' Jesus said. (And Judas the traitor was standing there with them.)
>
> When Jesus said, 'I am he,' they drew back and fell to the ground (John 18:4-6).

Jesus allowed the truth of who He is to be revealed in a physical way for just a moment, and there is enough power in Jesus' words that the guards and priests are knocked to the ground.

God's presence, His Spirit on earth, is not just a golden cloud floating around in the abstract. God is everywhere and in everything, but He specifically allows Himself to *BE* in one place in a greater measure to show us something of His nature. His Spirit is not a bunch of nice ideas and Bible verses. His Spirit has substance! It can fill you. And when it does, it affects you. Paul thought this was so important that He was constantly exhorting the church to "be filled" or "drink" in the Holy Spirit. "For we were all baptized by one Spirit so as to form one body—whether Jews or Gentiles, slave or free—and we were all given the one Spirit to drink" (1 Cor. 12:13).

Paul exhorts us, "Do not get drunk on wine, which leads to debauchery. Instead, be filled with the Spirit" (Eph. 5:18). I love this verse because it draws such a wonderful parallel between being filled with God's Spirit and getting drunk. Getting drunk on wine leads to debauchery; being filled with His Spirit leads to righteousness and all the other fruits of the Spirit. Jesus said, "But very truly I tell you, it is for your good that I am going away. Unless I go away, the Advocate will not come to you; but if I go, I will send him to you" (John 16:7).

Jesus knew that walking around in His physical body, He would never be able to have a personal and intimate encounter with every person on the planet. So He sent the Advocate, the one who would give the whole world access to the person of Jesus. The Holy Spirit is the one who highlights a Bible verse and makes it jump off the page at you. He is the one who was sent to teach us all things.

"But the Advocate, the Holy Spirit, whom the Father will send in my name, will teach you all things and will remind you of everything I have said to you" (John 14:26). This is the Spirit who was there at the beginning in Genesis hovering over the waters, ready to partner with God as He created all that we know today. The Advocate, as the Bible calls Him, is not God's sidekick or Jesus' assistant. He is one third of the trinity, the fullness of God come to earth to accomplish a specific purpose for His Glory. And that purpose is to encounter His people in an intimate and powerful way.

None of us could ever earn intimacy with God, "for all have sinned and fall short of the glory of God" (Rom. 3:23). But He bridged that gap! What we could not accomplish in our weakness, He did fully in His strength. He came and dwelt among us, Emmanuel Himself, so that He could Hold us like He held Mary as she wept at the tomb. He physically reached out and touched lepers for a reason! He was showing us His character. God will never stray away from us, despite our unclean state and our utter failure to uphold the Law. When we ask, He will come, and when He comes, He does so with *power,* always.

"Jesus Christ is the same yesterday, today and forever" (Heb. 13:8). As a church, we are called to believe that Jesus has not changed. God spent the whole Bible showing us story after story of Him dwelling amongst His people and drawing near to those whom He has called. You are called to live according to His purpose, and the only way to do that is by the power of His Spirit.

The purpose of this chapter is to show that God is passionate about encountering His children in *physical* ways. Every one of us who has chosen to follow Him has felt His touch in some way, but fears and expectations will threaten to quench any desire we may have for a physical encounter with Him.

The enemy makes us sick with diseases, fills our mind with lies and lays the weight of depression on some of us so heavily that we can't move. How much greater is the power of our God! His hand can touch your body and heal you! His voice can fill your mind with life-giving and encouraging thoughts! And He is fully capable of allowing the weight of His glory to rest upon you in such a way that you can't move!

At my job, many of our patients require transport two or three times a week. These people suffer from multiple illnesses and have little to no hope of recovery. One particular patient really caught my eye when I first started this job. I just knew that God had a special message for her hidden in my heart. So when I first received the call to transport her, I actually got excited and made sure I was the Tech riding in the back of the ambulance with her.

I was so excited to see what God was about to do, that I couldn't help but jump right in, "Ma'am, I have some really good news for you."

"What's that Josh?"

"You have a Father in heaven that really really loves you. We have never met, but every time I see you in a clinic, I have always felt this immense affection for you, and that is just a little overflow for how He feels about you."

Those words by themselves would have been nice, but I was not speaking under my own authority. When I said those words, the love of God flooded the back of the ambulance. She started to cry, and I began to feel the familiar weight and giddiness that so often accompanies the presence of God for me.

Through her tear, this sweet lady could only reply, "That's really nice, Josh. I feel good, real good. Thank you for saying that."

His touch is real and intimate. Without it, our hearts will always slip miserably into lukewarmness. It is when I become tired of backsliding, when the weight of despair has become too heavy on my heart, and I no longer have strength to resist His sweet invitation that He is there to wrap His arms around me. I invite you to pray this prayer with me, and see just how deep into His heart He wants to pull you:

God, your touch is a fundamental part of who I am. As your child, I need your support and strength as my Father. I repent for limiting who you are and what I think you will or won't do because of fear. I know you will never reject me, and as Your child, I ask that You would come and surround me right now with your presence. Teach me what it means to be close to you and show me what life would look like with you filling me. I do not ask these things for my sake, but for the sake of Your Son who left so that I might experience you fully through the Holy Spirit.

"If you then, though you are evil, know how to give good gifts to your children, how much more will your Father in heaven give the Holy Spirit to those who ask him!" (Luke 11:13).

Chapter Eight
Through His Body

"And I heard a sound from heaven like the roar of rushing waters and like a loud peal of thunder. The sound I heard was like that of harpists playing their harps" (Rev. 14:2).

      God speaks in so many beautiful ways, and it is our joy to fall deep into the waters of His love and be filled with the thunderous power of His glory. We were never meant to experience this fullness alone. We were made to experience the fullness of God's love in community, side by side with brothers and sisters who hold us up when we would otherwise fall.

      The concept of a unified church is both the great failing of our forefathers and the great promise of the coming generation. We were crafted to function in a family, and when the enemy successfully isolates us, we miss out on great portions of our inheritance, rendering us completely inert. The character of Jesus' love is wide, deep, powerful and mysterious and it will take every living believer to fully embody His person on earth.

      In order to properly display His Son, God has developed this ingenious "Body of Christ" that manifests community and family as offshoots of its nature. In this body, we are all given different callings and gifts in the Holy Spirit that we were meant to share amongst each other in love, and in sharing, be made complete and mature:

> "Now to each one the manifestation of the Spirit is given for the common good." (1 Cor. 12:7)

We all have the same Holy Spirit, who gives us full access to the riches of heaven through Jesus. "Praise be to the God and Father of our Lord Jesus Christ, who has blessed us in the heavenly realms with every spiritual blessing in Christ. (Eph. 1:3)

Yet each of us only knows a part of the whole of Jesus. He reserves the full revelations of His character for the whole body, not just one individual. Even Paul, arguably the greatest theologian to ever live, said, "...now I know in part; then I shall know fully, even as I am fully known" (1 Cor. 13:12).

God created a system of interdependence so that the body could grow up in maturity while abounding in humility. No one man has been given headship; instead, Jesus is the Head of all. The Holy Spirit is teaching us all things, and we all have received the beautiful gift of direct relationship with Y-H-W-H through Jesus Christ. In this way, we have received the full measure of the promise described in Hebrews. "No longer will they teach their neighbor, or say to one another, 'Know the Lord,' because they will all know me, from the least of them to the greatest" (Heb. 8:11).

Yet as we come together as a broken and humbled body of believers, we can only be built up into the mature bride we were made to be one way.

> "What then shall we say, brothers and sisters? When you come together, each of you has a hymn, or a word of instruction, a revelation, a tongue or an interpretation. Everything must be done so that the church may be built up" (1 Cor. 14:26).

Notice how exact the language is. It does not say "*some* of you have a hymn, or a word." It says, "*each* [emphasis added] of you has a hymn, or a word." Then again, it does not say, "as long as *most* of you share, the church will be built up." It says, "Everything must be done so that the church may be built up."

I surrendered my life to Jesus and received the power of the Holy Spirit. This started me on a radical and wonderful adventure of love. I can hear the voice of my Creator, and He leads me to do some risky things, but He never leaves me out to dry. He meets me every time, turning all things out for my good and showing up in power. There is nothing unique about the nature of my calling. Each of us is called to participate in the great calling of the Bride of Christ.

"It was for this He called you through our gospel, that you may gain the glory of our Lord Jesus Christ" (2 Thess. 2:14). There is a reason we were all called to pursue the glory of Jesus Christ. God knew we would need each other! Some of the most memorable and impactful revelations I have ever received from the Holy Spirit came through another believer, usually in a way I did not expect or from a source I had to grow in humility to receive from.

This is the way the physical body works. Each cell receives its identity from the DNA, an indwelling presence that holds within itself instructions for the whole body. Each cell listens to its DNA and behaves as it was made to. Cells are susceptible and weak by themselves; they are easily fooled by viruses. If a certain group of cells is wounded too many times, it can begin to think that reproducing its specific nature is all that matters. These cells become malignant cancer.

Our brilliant designer created cells to function in groups that interact with other cell groups for the benefit of the whole. If a virus comes into the body and is deceiving a cell group, the immune system will release special t-cells to literally cover over the weakness of the targeted cells and reject the virus.

All of these wonderful functions of our body are just signs pointing the the healthy function of our united spiritual body. I have personally been saved from "viruses" many times by other "cells" in the body through God's intervention, "because the Lord disciplines the one he loves, and he chastens everyone he accepts as his son" (Heb. 12:6).

Disciplining myself is a challenge, and if the Lord wants to correct me in love, He sometimes uses the voice of another to do so. Now, just like any other facet of the Lord's voice, I always look for confirmation in the Scripture and in the counsel of my elders. But the reality is, even though it can be fairly uncomfortable to be corrected or rebuked by someone in the body, God is using these vessels to steer you in the right direction. Especially, when you think the person is unqualified. Imagine how Balaam felt when he was rebuked by God through the mouth of a donkey! (Num. 22). It is through submitting and listening to my elders and peers that I have even made it this far in Christianity. And I know that to abandon this route of hearing God's voice is to abandon the safety net God put in place to catch me when I am being deceived.

I have had numerous friends who came to Christ in radical and wonderful ways, only to fall away a year or two later. They were ministering, reading the Bible and evangelizing, yet they still fell away. There was no difference between my calling and theirs. They received the same invitation from Jesus, but they never understood that following Jesus was about more than just their personal walks with Him.

Sadly, I have seen this pattern played out several times over the years. Someone gets radically impacted by the Lord and becomes extremely passionate about the kingdom. Then when the initial excitement wears off and they find themselves face to face with their own brokenness. They refuse to face it. They cover over it with works or by becoming even louder and more passionate. All the while, the secret sin grows in the dark. These things left unconfessed and hidden become the root of their eventual downfall. No matter how much we mature in Christ, we can never outgrow our brokenness. Brokenness in the context of community can become the doorway to greater humility and hunger. But if we allow that brokenness to lead us away from our brothers and sisters, hiding the true state of our hearts, we doom ourselves to a one-on-one fight with the enemy, a fight we were not designed to win.

No one has ever followed Jesus alone, and there are no "lone-wolves" in the Bible. Having a relationship with Jesus and receiving the "words of life" Peter talks about in John 6:68 has always included living out life in a community of believers. To truly understand and grow in intimacy with God on His terms, we must, "submit to one another out of reverence for Christ" (Eph. 5:21).

Much of the time, when people talk about, "hearing directly from God," the prevailing fear is of deception from the enemy. All of us have, at one point or another, met someone who is completely isolated in their faith and, as a result, has come to believe some very bizarre and skewed things about the nature of God's character and his commandments. God gave us a safeguard in this arena! The key to avoiding deception is not to avoid the issue of God's voice altogether, but to pursue it surrounded by a loving community!

Whether we like it or not, we are a nation of believers engaged in a war with the kingdom of darkness. "For lack of guidance a nation falls, but victory is won through many advisers" (Prov. 11:14).

This concept in the Old Testament is taken from metaphor to specific application in the area of hearing God's voice in 1 Corinthians. "For you can all prophesy in turn so that everyone may be instructed and encouraged. The spirits of prophets are subject to the control of prophets. For God is not a God of disorder but of peace—as in all the congregations of the Lord's people" (1 Cor. 14:31-33).

Paul lays it out so simply here! Everyone can prophesy, and should, for the encouragement and instruction of the church. All that is said will then be weighed and either accepted by the body or if error is found, corrected in a loving and oftentime private manner.

The reality is we cannot follow Jesus at all without the guidance and teaching of the Holy Spirit, and even in that, we will all make mistakes. To expect to be perfectly obedient to Jesus without some sort of process of failure is foolish. We are not left to face the consequences of our mistakes alone. We have been given a community of brothers and sisters for this very reason! "Above all, love each other deeply, because love covers over a multitude of sins" (1 Pet. 4:8).

Find the community Holy Spirit has set aside for you to walk out your faith in, and "submit to each other in love." You will save yourself so much unnecessary hurt and confusion in this world. Pray this prayer with me to open our hearts further to the revelation, love and correction that God has provided for us in our brothers and sisters:

Jesus, I submit myself fully to you. Soften my heart to receive instruction, no matter its source. I ask that you give me the humility to follow in your path of radical vulnerability towards others as you sought the voice of Your Father in all that you did. Holy Spirit, come and instruct me in wisdom, teaching me to fear Your name and rely on Your faithfulness. I open myself to the wise counsel and loving encouragement that You have for me in the brothers and sisters you have placed in my life. Amen

Chapter Nine
Being Like Jesus

"Therefore be imitators of God, as beloved children. And walk in love, as Christ loved us and gave himself up for us, a fragrant offering and sacrifice to God" (Eph. 5:1-2).

Jesus was the kernel of wheat that God planted in the ground of this broken world (John 12:24). No one has ever planted a bunch of apple seeds and hoped for plums. No! A seed is only planted for one reason: to reproduce the fruit from which it came. Hidden in Jesus is the blueprint for the production of all the fruits of the Spirit described in the Bible.

"For you died, and your life is now hidden with Christ in God" (Col. 3:3). No matter who you are or what you do, you have been called. Your pastor or favorite Christian author cannot show you the plans God has for your life. They cannot tell you the wonderful and sweet ways He wants you to love the people around you. As Paul describes, "these are the things God has revealed to us by his Spirit. The Spirit searches all things, even the deep things of God" (1 Cor. 2:10).

We were designed to be living and thriving extensions of God's love on the planet. The key to this design was hidden in the life and words of Jesus Christ, and it is from this perfect seed, we have all grown. "For you have been born again, not of perishable seed, but of imperishable, through the living and enduring word of God" (1 Pet. 1:23).

God is reproducing His son through your life right now! No matter where you are in the process, the Holy Spirit is working to manifest Christ in your life. To this end, He has surrounded and filled you with His voice. He is displaying His characteristics in the reckless beauty of nature. He shows Himself in the kindness of strangers and and in the depth and mystery of the Scripture. He is revealing Himself for all to see, so that in the seeing, we may become like what we behold!

I am a man surrounded by the love and affection of a wonderful Father. At every turn, I encounter the encouragement and delight I have inherited through the blood of Christ. His voice permeates my marriage and gently pulls me into His arms when I fail. I am not a full-time minister nor do I hold any official position in ministry. I am simply a son loved by his Father. This love that saturates my life does not make me perfect but covers over my imperfections with grace.

No place is this more true than in my workplace. I am a full time EMT and spend twelve hours, four days a week with some of the most broken and helpless people in our country. While I am at work, I am not a walking billboard for holiness, yet by His mercy, I am constantly being followed by the fruits of the Spirit. I cannot help but be obedient as I hear the still quiet voice invite me to do all sorts of risky things in the back of ambulances. I have prayed for patients on death's door and seen them recover. I have told special brothers and sisters about our heavenly father in tears and seen them encounter His love. I face the misery of despair and the ravages of sin on the human body everyday and yet I rejoice.

In the face of such darkness, I need a weapon more powerful than what I heard in the sermon last sunday. I need the lamp upon my feet, the One who will *teach me all things*. Our access to the voice of our Father can no longer be limited by fear of deception or reserved for the "few anointed chosen" of our generation.

Jesus is coming back very soon, and we must be ready. We must be ready like the ten virgins in Matthew 25. The oil in this parable represents the anointing and presence of the Holy Spirit's ministry in our lives. We are called to know and be known by God. We cannot do this without a powerful and daily connection with God through the Holy Spirit.

I am praying for our generation to truly lay hold of what was given to us in Christ Jesus! I can think of no better way to end this book than with the words of Paul:

> I pray that the eyes of your heart may be enlightened in order that you may know the hope to which he has called you, the riches of his glorious inheritance in his holy people, and his incomparably great power for us who believe. That power is the same as the mighty strength he exerted when he raised Christ from the dead and seated him at his right hand in the heavenly realms, far above all rule and authority, power and dominion, and every name that is invoked, not only in the present age but also in the one to come. And God placed all things under his feet and appointed him to be head over everything for the church, which is his body, the fullness of him who fills everything in every way (Eph. 1:18-23).
>
> *Amen.*

Chapter Ten

What now?

"Instead, speaking the truth in love, we will grow to become in every respect the mature body of him who is the head, that is, Christ" (Eph. 4:15).

If you take anything away from this book, I want it to be: **Hearing from the Lord is easy!**

He has truly made Himself utterly accessible through the sacrifice of His son Jesus Christ. Yet even though we have been given everything in Jesus Christ, there is an undeniable process of sanctification each of us go through as we grow in maturity as His body. For the sake of this book, I will define sanctification as the process of learning obedience through suffering, taking on the very nature of Christ to share in His glory for eternity. The Scripture is clear that we each must endure His suffering in order to share in His glory. We do not earn anything from Him, but in order to mature as His children, we are called to walk the same path as His Son.

"Now if we are children, then we are heirs -- heirs of God and co-heirs with Christ, if indeed we share in his sufferings in order that we may also share in his glory" (Rom. 8:17). Even Jesus "...learned obedience from what he suffered" (Heb. 5:8).

God gives the gift of His voice without repentance, and I honestly believe that He is willing to talk to anybody. This may seem like a bold assertion, but I am hardpressed to find a category of person who Jesus would not humble himself to speak to directly. He spoke to the adulterous woman at the well, something that was extremely taboo at the time (John 4). He spoke to an unrepentant Saul and completely redirected the path of his life (Acts 9:4). He spoke to the Canaanite woman, someone He specified was not an inheritor of His ministry (Matt. 15). So no matter what you think disqualifies you from hearing the voice of the Lord, "Ask and it will be given to you; seek and you will find; knock and the door will be opened to you" (Matt. 7:7).

So freely we are given access to the voice of the Lord through the blood of Jesus, but what does it mean to mature in this area of our walk with Him? I believe maturity in the realm of hearing God's voice manifests in two main areas. The first is the ability to *share* something God has been showing you in love. The second is to *learn* patience and obedience with things God shows you, always waiting on His perfect timing.

When I first started dating my wife, I went around asking many of my elders and peers for advice on how to maintain a healthy relationship. While I got all sorts of answers, they all emphasized the importance of communication -- whether it was the casual comment: "communication is key" or some deeper insight like: "Right now, you speak different languages. Learning the way each other communicates is one of the most important things you will do in your relationship." Communication was constantly brought up as something that could make or break a relationship.

As I have grown in my relationship with my wife, I have only begun to discover the depths of the value of hearing her voice and understanding what she is really saying. For example, when my wife asks me to go on a walk, she is not looking for a silent exercise partner; she is looking for an emotional connection with her husband in her favorite setting. Because I have grown to understand what her heart is longing for, I cannot just fulfill her request with my physical presence. Instead, I truly make an effort to reach out with my heart and offer her the connection she desires.

This simple wisdom is deeply applicable to our relationship with Jesus. At some point, we each begin a conversation with Him that will last the rest of our life. Learning to recognize His voice in all its forms is a wonderful lesson each of us are guided through by the Holy Spirit. But the lesson does not stop at simply receiving His thoughts towards you or others. He wants to take you deeper! Behind every word God speaks is the deeper reality of His heart! In fact, the purpose of His voice is to reveal His heart. Jesus showed us this principle when He said, "For the mouth speaks what the heart is full of" (Luke 6:45).

This concept is key for us who are seeking out the voice of the Lord. God's heart is behind everything He says. And the less we know His heart, the less we understand the meaning of what He shows to us. For example, I have a deep compassion for men and women stuck in the cycle of pornography and masturbation. God met me in that place of my weakness and washed me clean in love, not just once but many times, showing me that there is greater intimacy and more abundant pleasure available at His right hand.

That being said, there are times in the past where I have been sitting next to some guy and God has said, "*That is my Son next to you, and he is addicted to porn. I want Him to be free.*" For some people, hearing that secret about someone would be a terrible burden. Anxiety and fear would dominate the internal conversation of their hearts.

"Do I have to confront Him?"

"How do I bring something like this up?"

"I probably shouldn't say anything at all. It's not my place."

This has actually happened to me many times, and everytime God fills me with more peace and joy than the time before. Why? Because I am intimately familiar with God's heart in this matter. He is not concerned with the sin itself — that was dealt with on the Cross. Instead, His main focus for that person, for me, is to communicate love and hope. The love of God is a love that will overwhelm shame because He brings a hope that continues to shine, no matter how dark life gets. He will always come through for those who ask, no matter the sin.

When He tells me something like this, I am filled with hope and joy. I know the only reason God reveals a dark place in someone's heart is because He is about to do something about it. He rescued me, and I know there is not a single person He will leave drowning in this struggle, as long as there is at least one person interceding by the blood of Jesus for breakthrough. Because I know God's heart behind these words, I can begin to pray in faith for that person or sometimes even bring up the subject. Whatever I do, I strive to do in love just like Paul stated in Ephesians 4:15.

It is this longing to share the truth in love that has led me to seek the wisdom of the Lord in regards to His timing, and the context in which He desires to share truth. Hearing the Lord's voice is such a gift, but hearing Him is not the end of the journey; it's just the beginning! Even if it costs us all we have, we are called to get understanding! We must grow in the intimate understanding of our Creator's heart, so that when He speaks, each word is deeply rooted in the context of His love and propelled forward by His endless passion. "The beginning of wisdom is this: Get wisdom. Though it cost all you have, get understanding" (Prov. 4:7).

He is not shallow and He has never spoken an idle word. I on the other hand still do all the time! We are so different, and His ways are so much higher than mine. I mean, honestly, I am still trying to understand what He really means when He says, *"Son, I love you, and I am so pleased with you."*

Luckily, we are not left to find this all out on our own; instead, we have a wonderful Counselor—the Holy Spirit. "These are the things God has revealed to us by his Spirit. The

Spirit searches all things, even the deep things of God" (1 Cor. 2:10).

It is in the depth of God's heart that we will find the joy of His timing. He is undeniably a God of perfect timing. In every promise and every season of waiting, we are constantly being challenged to gain a deeper trust and understanding of His timing. "The Lord is not slow in keeping his promise, as some understand slowness. Instead he is patient with you, not wanting anyone to perish, but everyone to come to repentance" (2 Pet. 3:9).

When the Lord led me to give my first car away, He said, "Son, I will replace this care with your dream car, so spend time researching and I will give you whatever car you choose." At the time, I had no money, but nonetheless, I took God at His word and chose the car I wanted, a Forest Green 1999 Subaru Forester.

After several discouraging exchanges, I had decided that maybe I should start broadening my horizons and look at other cars. Then I found the exact car I was looking for on Craigslist! The only downside was that the engine was dead and the owner had no idea why. I had $650 at the time and they sold it to me for that much.

I then had it towed to garage after garage to see how much it would cost to fix. After three different quotes, I had gotten the cost down to $2500, money I did not have, so I got the car towed to my dad's driveway and waited. I hooked up the car battery to our house and began to pray and worship in the car with the radio. Although this seems like something small, the process was very frustrating for me. I felt like God was always taking me by the hardest route to give me His promises. Even so, I would sit in my dead car and tell God I loved Him and trusted His plan.

One month later, I found a man who was willing to replace my dead engine with his 1999 Forester engine for only $1200. Once again, the exact amount I had saved up to that point. That was about two years ago, and it has been a great car ever since.

God is a huge fan of waiting. He knows so many wonderful things happen when we trust in Him and have to wait on the fulfillment of His promises. I mean, the Bible is absolutely stuffed full of blessings for anyone waiting on the Lord. Here are just a couple to wet your whistle:

> Yet the LORD longs to be gracious to you; therefore he will rise up to show you compassion. For the LORD is a God of justice. Blessed are all who wait for him!" (Isa. 30:18).

> In the morning, O LORD, You will hear my voice; In the morning I will order my prayer to You and eagerly watch" (Ps. 5:3).

Even though we each experience a wonderful rhythm of highs and lows when we wait on our Father, I don't know many people who would say they enjoy waiting. In fact, I would say that waiting is pretty much torture in our own strength. Nothing has filled me with more uncertainty and fear than certain periods of waiting in my life, but as I have gotten to know God, this has begun to completely change! Now as I am invited to believe for more and more impossible things, such promises are not burdens that I carry on my shoulders, but beacons of hope that shine in my thinking, filling me with faith. The Lord has promised that He will save every one of my coworkers, and I have actually begun to see some of them be drawn into the kingdom!

Now that I am hanging out in the vine, I have access to endless patience and joy. With Him, every day of waiting is a day of increased hope and anticipation. And then in the fullness of timing, when I can receive His promise in the fullest way possible, He comes through. Always!

It is for this very reason that I believe Jesus has not come back yet. The father is waiting for the church to fulfill its destiny as His bride. Once we have grown into the mature and spotless bride that the Father has promised His son, He will be sent to meet us and claim the earth as His inheritance. Yet this period of waiting that we find ourselves in right now is not permission for passivity. He is inviting us to passionately wait for the coming of His Son and the fulfillment of every one of His promises.

No place is this more true than the realm of His voice. He will give you so many promises- it is ridiculous! If you let Him, He will drown every relationship and situation in your life with promises. Why does He do this? Because He knows He can and will come through for those who wait on Him. So many things He tells you will not be for today or tomorrow but for years and sometimes even generations to come. When He told Abraham that he would be a father of many nations, He was trusting Abraham with a promise that would not be fulfilled for thousands of years!

Such a calling to believe even when we don't see is not a weight or heavy burden for us. I mean, our whole spiritual history is filled with amazing pioneers who had the faith to believe for promises they would not inherit in their lifetime. Again, Abraham was a trusted keeper of so many promises that to this day shape our beliefs and experiences as Christians! "For he (Abraham) was looking forward to the city with foundations, whose architect and builder is God" (Heb. 11:10).

God uses waiting and testing to form us into the image of His Son. Times of testing are gifts, not burdens. They establish trust and deepen aspects of our relationship with God, and by extension, His voice. As you grow with Him, you will receive so much! His heart is truly endless, and His thoughts towards you are as many as the sands on the seashore. In fact, you can know you are in a healthy communication rhythm with God when most of the conversation is made up of you listening and Him speaking.

I want to leave you with this encouragement I believe the Lord is speaking over each one of you:

My son, my daughter, I love you. I am so glad you have come to this place with me, and I want you to know I am inviting you into a deeper place in my heart. I will show you the secrets of my Covenant and unlock the power inherent in my Son's blood. I have chosen you because I love you, and I want to reveal Myself in a new and powerful way through your life. Come meet me in the cleft of the rock and let me whisper secret and wonderful things in your ear. For my Son is coming back very soon, and I want you to be ready.

Come on. Let's get you ready to meet your Husband.

Learn more about the Author at:

joshuahutto.com

Made in the USA
Middletown, DE
26 September 2017